Pirates of Southwest Florida

Pirates of Southwest Florida

✦

Fact and Legend

James F. and Sarah Jane Kaserman

iUniverse, Inc.
New York Lincoln Shanghai

Pirates of Southwest Florida
Fact and Legend

iUniverse books may be ordered through booksellers or by contacting:

iUniverse
2021 Pine Lake Road, Suite 100
Lincoln, NE 68512
www.iuniverse.com
1-800-Authors (1-800-288-4677)

Because of the dynamic nature of the Internet, any Web addresses or links contained in this book may have changed since publication and may no longer be valid.

The views expressed in this work are solely those of the author and do not necessarily reflect the views of the publisher, and the publisher hereby disclaims any responsibility for them.

ISBN: 978-0-595-47152-2 (pbk)
ISBN: 978-0-595-91432-6 (ebk)

Printed in the United States of America

Contents

Introduction vii

CHAPTER 1   The Two Black Caesars of Sanibel and Captiva
             Islands 1

CHAPTER 2   Famous Pirates Honeymooned on Lover's Key 5

CHAPTER 3   The Legend of Gasparilla 9

CHAPTER 4   The FACTS About The Gasparilla Legend 13

CHAPTER 5   Brewster Baker, Legendary Pirate, a Legendary
             Name 16

CHAPTER 6   John Gomez, A Living Legend Who Created
             Legends 19

CHAPTER 7   Lafitte's Treasures and Other Treasure Legends of
             Southwest Florida 23

CHAPTER 8   Blockade Runners and the Development of
             Southwest Florida during the Civil War 29

CHAPTER 9   From Civil War Through Prohibition 33

CHAPTER 10   From Prohibition Until Today 37

Glossary 41

Bibliography 47

About the Authors 49

Introduction

Nearly twenty centuries have passed since pirates captured Julius Caesar in 78 B.C. and he became one of the first people ever held for ransom in recorded history. Piracy historically has occurred anywhere there is commerce, including lakes, rivers, and oceans. In the United States, some of the most brutal pirates were known as the "Ohio River Pirates" and operated for decades from Cave-in-Rock, which is now a state park in Illinois.

Piracy, in many forms, continues to this day and will be a formidable future challenge in some areas of the world. From traditional acts of piracy through human smuggling, billions of dollars of plunder annually are gained by pirates worldwide today! 1

Over the past three centuries, many songs, plays, poems, films, and literature have formed romantic ideals and stereotypes about pirates. Pirates left few written records, as it was not in their best interests, since these written accounts could be used against them in a court of law. The art, woodcuts, and engravings that allege to show pirates are as phony as the many tales of buried treasures. 2

Many historical accounts of piracy seem as impossible as to sound like fiction and many mythical accounts seem so real as to be factual. As an example of an historical event, Alwilda was the daughter of a Scandinavian king in the fifth century A.D. As was custom, her father had arranged for her to marry Prince Alf, the son of Sygarus, King of Denmark, but she was so opposed that she and some of her female friends dressed up as men, found a ship, and befriended some male pirates who elected her captain. Under her command, she became a formidable pirate force in the Baltic Sea. Prince Alf was dispatched to hunt down these pirates. A fierce naval battle took place in the Gulf of Finland, during which time Prince Alf and his men boarded the pirate vessel killed most of her crew and took Alwilda prisoner. Alwilda was so impressed with Prince Alf's fighting abilities that she changed her mind and was persuaded to accept his hand in marriage. They were married on board his ship and she eventually became Queen of Denmark. 3

Some other facts concerning pirates that the reader should know to enjoy our book include the following:

- The Colonists in the Revolutionary War employed pirates and private ship owners as "Privateers" to fight the British Navy issued over 3,000 "Letters of Marque". Privateers!

- The invention of the steam engine and large national navies ended the *"golden age"* of piracy. The American "mosquito fleet" chased pirates from U.S.A.

- Pirate Confederations were among the only true democracies ever formed and elected their captains, shared prizes equally, and formed a basis for our original Articles of Confederation

- Piracy believed in equal rights and led to end of slave trade. At any given time in history, between 30 and 50 percent of pirates were black.

- Some famous pirates were women and influenced history. Grace O'Malley or Granuaile, the Irish pirate, is the most influential to history. Cheng I Sao or Ching Shih was the ruler of largest navy in the world at its time, the Red Fleet, with over 1,000 ships. Anne Bonny, born in Ireland, but who lived in Charleston, South Carolina, along with Mary Read, were the most famous American women pirates. Lovers Key is named by/for Anne Bonny and Calico Jack Rackham

- Pirates were performance based organizations who had written and strict codes of conduct ("Honor Among Thieves") **"Parleys"** were another term for trials by juries of one's peers

- Pirates discovered various forms of insurance we use today. 4.

Our first chapter will look at Henri Caesar, known as Black Caesar, who plied the waters of Sanibel Island and Key Largo in the period of 1680—1718. He was the first well-known pirate of what became known as "The Mangrove Coast" of Florida.

---

1.   Raffaele, Paul, The Pirate Hunters, <u>Smithsonian,</u> August, 2007.

2. Cordingly, David, *Under the Black Flag*, Random House, New York, New York, 1995.

3. Rediker, Marcus, *Villains of All Nations*, Beacon Press, Boston, MA, 2004.

4. Kaserman, James F., "Truth About Pirates" Presentations, 2001—2007.

1

The Two Black Caesars of Sanibel and Captiva Islands

Not one; but TWO famous black pirates lived on Sanibel and Captiva Islands. This is not surprising, because in the 17th and 18th centuries, as many as 30% of all sailors were of African descent. Black sailors were sought for many jobs at sea including cooks, musicians, and skilled sailors. It is estimated that nearly 50% of Caribbean pirates were black during the same time frame. During the "Golden Age of Piracy" (1680-1725) Africans were often forced to work as slaves on land. But on the sea they were treated as equals.

Ironically both pirates claimed the same name and came from similar backgrounds before becoming feared pirate captains. Their names were Henri Caesar or Black Caesar. It is probable that the latter Black Caesar took his pirate name from the earlier one. Both were involved with the legends of imprisoning women on Captiva Island.

The first Black Caesar was an African chief known for his intelligence, leadership ability, and physical strength. In Africa, he became involved with the slave trade with his tribe providing many slaves to the slave traders. Both he and his tribe became wealthy and powerful. The slavers, finding it hard to financially deal with the chief, tricked Black Caesar onto a slave ship where they imprisoned him and shipped him to the Spanish Main. Enroute, a severe hurricane struck the slave ship. Caesar and others escaped from the sinking ship and attached themselves to remnants of the ship, floating to what is now Adams Key, on the southern tip of Elliot Key in the eastern upper Florida Keys.

Black Caesar and his pirate band of former slaves established a pirate community and began a very successful period of attacking and capturing merchantmen and small boats of all nations. Legend has it that these early pirates, operating in the Florida Keys, would bring their prey and captured ships back to what is now known as "Caesar's Rock." There they would tie the ships to the rock and sink them in order to effectively hide their treasures. Although he established a prison on Elliott Key he was brutal to his captives. This Black Caesar is given historic credit for first using the phrase, "dead men tell no tales."

The first Black Caesar enjoyed women and some historians estimate that he had over 100 women in his harem and prison camp on Elliott Key. Black Caesar decided to move his harem out of harm's way and away from threats from his own pirates to the current islands of Sanibel and Captiva. He built a village for his women on what became known as Captiva Island. He established a base on Sanibel Island and traded actively with the Calusa Indians from what is now Pine Island.

Black Caesar moved between Sanibel-Captiva and the islands to Elliott Key for a number of years during this period. Black Caesar joined forces with one of the most notorious pirates, Blackbeard. They were together in 1718 when Blackbeard's ship was attacked and captured. Both were tried and hanged in Williamsburg, Virginia.

One hundred years later another Black Caesar came into Southwest Florida history. The second Black Caesar was historically one of the most vicious pirates that plied the waters of Southwest Florida and the Spanish Main. Caesar was born in 1767, the son of slaves owned by Monsieur Arnaut, a wealthy planter with a large plantation on Hispanola. Very intelligent, at a young age, Caesar became a houseboy and enjoyed a good life. He learned a great deal from his master's conversations. He was exposed to the better things in life and developed a burning desire to not only be free but to become a free gentleman.

Unfortunately for Caesar, by age16, he had grown to over six feet and become a physical specimen. Arnaut had him placed in the plantation lumberyard where his strength could be better utilized. Caesar resented this transfer, which was a drop in his status from the good food and easy tasks enjoyed by the domestic house servants.

Worse yet, the lumberyard overseer was a cruel Frenchman who loved to whip the slaves and draw blood from the them while they were cutting mahogany logs with two man saws, 12 hours a day, 6 days a week. Hatred of this man became paramount in the young Caesar's mind. Caesar took part in plans to revolt and, in 1791, joined Boukman Dutty and others to free the slaves from their masters. He took great joy in killing his cruel overseer with the very saw he was forced to use, virtually cutting him to pieces. He then spent 9 years as a leader in the jungles attacking French patrols and forts. In 1804, France gave up the country and Haiti became the first nation in the Western Hemisphere to become independent after the United States. Caesar was disgusted with the lack of planning and government by the revolution leaders and turned to pirating out of Port de Paix on the northern coast.

After capturing ships off Cuba and the Bahamas, Caesar realized that relocating to Elliott Key in the Florida Keys would give his pirates a great location to attack small merchant ships off the Cuban coast and the Bahamas Channel. Like the first Caesar, this Black Caesar and his pirates were successful for the next decade. He began to refer to himself as Caesar the Great.

However, following the War of 1812 and the purchase of Florida by the United States, Black Caesar was forced to abandon his lucrative base on Elliott Key and move northwestward into the Gulf of Mexico. He established camps on most of the now populated islands off the Southwest Florida coast, including Marco Island, Black Island, Sanibel Island, Captiva Island, and Pine Island. These camps gave impetus to many false tales of buried treasure.

Black Caesar or Caesar le Grande established a settlement on the bay side of Sanibel Island and did carry on pirate raids against small villages and small ships off the coast of Florida and Cuba. During this time period, Black Caesar brought back prisoners for ransom and, just as his namesake is alleged to have done 100 years earlier, is thought to have placed his female captives on Captiva Island.

The legend of the second Black Caesar includes his overtures to join Jose Gaspar, known as Gasparilla, whose actual existence is doubted by most historians. Part of this legend includes the fact that Gasparilla, rumored to be a true, old-world "gentleman" never liked Caesar. When some of Black Caesar's men allegedly became drunk and attacked many of Gasparilla's female captives on Captiva Island, it is said that Gasparilla's pirates drove Black Caesar from Sanibel and Captiva Islands.

Black Caesar began drinking heavily and suffered the lapses of judgment tied to such actions. He was captured by the Spanish off the coast of Cuba in 1829 and died shortly after his capture.

2

Famous Pirates Honeymooned on Lover's Key

John "Calico Jack" Rackham and Anne Bonny are two of the most famous 18th century pirates in recorded history. Their relationship and careers were short-lived; but, the time they spent on Estero Island and Lover's Key has forever tied their names to Southwest Florida history.

Calico Jack Rackham, although a successful pirate captain, is more noted for the colorful calico cotton clothes he wore, when most other pirates of the time dressed in rich silks and velvets. Captain Jack is also noted for having two famous female pirates as members of his crew.

In 1718, John Rackham had been the quartermaster, generally second in command, on an English flagged warship, the Neptune, under the command of Captain Charles Vane. After engaging a French warship, Captain Vane ordered the Neptune to retreat and withdraw from further fighting. The Neptune's crew objected and voted to make John Rackham the new captain. Vane was abandoned on an island and Rackham took over the helm.

The Neptune was renamed Kingston and Rackham and his crew spent the next several months successfully attacking smaller ships and keeping the booty. In early 1719, England and Spain renewed their conflicts and "Calico Jack" Rackham sailed to Jamaica in the hopes of being given a pardon or commission. After a Spanish warship attacked his ship, he and most of his crew were able to escape by stealing two fishing vessels. When the Kingston was reclaimed by the Spanish, Rackham was forced to sea in the two smaller boats, from which they captured a Spanish sloop off Cuba, and sailed it to New Providence in the Bahamas. Woodes Rogers, the governor, granted him a pardon in the late spring of 1719. It was there that he first met Anne Bonny, the wife of another lesser-known pirate, James Bonny.

Anne Bonny was born in 1697 in County Cork, Ireland. She was the red-haired daughter of a servant woman, Mary or Peg Brennan, and a famous lawyer, William Cormac. William's wife discovered the affair and exposed it publicly. In disgrace, William Cormac, Mary or Peg Brennan, and baby Anne fled the scandal and sailed to settle in Charleston, South Carolina. Anne's parents became wealthy merchants and plantation owners in the New World.

When Anne reached the age of 12, at that time considered a marriageable age, she had many suitors. In addition to being rich and beautiful, it is significant that Anne had a violent temper. She stabbed a servant girl with a knife and severely beat a boy who made advances towards her. Anne then chose to run off and marry James Bonny, a renegade pirate and sometime merchant seaman. Worried that James Bonny would attempt to steal his vast land holdings, Anne's father, Michael Cormac, publicly disowned his daughter.

The Bonny newlyweds moved to New Providence, and it was there that this stunning Irish beauty met Calico Jack Rackham. They began an affair that was soon discovered by Anne's husband. James Bonny seized his bride and brought her naked before Governor Woodes Rogers, charging her with the then felony offense of deserting him. Anne was considered to be stolen property, and it was common for the governor to put the offender up for public sale to the highest bidder. Instead, Calico Jack suggested that he would buy Anne directly from her husband. James Bonny protested and got a court order forbidding Anne and Calico Jack to even see one another. Rackham decided the only way he could have his lover was to return to the pirate life.

Jack and Anne escaped the authorities along with a couple of Rackham's former pirates and stole one of the fastest ships in the harbor, the Curlew. This ship was taken at midnight under Anne Bonny's leadership where she confronted the two men on board and threatened to blow their brains out if they offered any resistance.

Jack Rackham and Anne Bonny began the cruise that they called their honeymoon by attacking smaller ships off the coast of Cuba and successfully selling their prizes. Anne was a fierce fighter and superior to most of the men on board the ship. Trouble began when they attacked a Spanish sloop near Key West. In the ensuing battle, their mainmast was shattered so that a new mast needed to be found and installed. A storm then blew the stricken ship north into the Gulf of Mexico and up the coast to a place off Estero Island. After finding deep water on the southern end of Estero Island and present day Lover's Key, they guided their ship to safe anchorage. In longboats, the members of the crew rowed up the Estero River and found many tall trees sufficient to be carved into a mast and spars. According to Johnson's "History of Highwaymen and Pyrates," published in London in 1818, 'while the ship's carpenter and crew did labour mightily to refit the vessel, Calico Jack and the woman, Anne Bonny, did make merry for many days on the island where they had a dwelling made of sticks and palms.' Considering that nine months after this visit to what is now Lover's Key, the couple had their first child, it is safe to say that Lover's Key is appropriately named.

Following the Curlew's repairs in Southwest Florida, the pirate couple continued attacking Spanish ships near Cuba. Anne was now blossoming with child and Calico Jack took her to Cuba where the baby was born. Since Anne loved life as a pirate on the sea, she soon left their first born with an older couple that were former pirates, and returned to pirating.

Upon Anne's return, Calico Jack and his crew attacked and captured a Dutch ship off Cuba. As was custom, a number of the Dutch crew were forced to sign articles (a pirate contract) or be imprisoned and sold off at slave markets. One of these handsome young Dutch boys was neither Dutch nor a boy. Anne was drawn to the newcomer and Calico Jack became jealous. He was shocked to discover that the young Dutch boy was really an English woman by the name of Mary Read. Mary Read was born illegitimately and her mother had raised her as a boy. In fact, Mary Read fought heroically in Flanders as an English dragoon in the War of Spanish Succession.

These two women became legendary because of their courage and bravery during many battles and encounters undertaken by Calico Jack and the pirates on board the Revenge, the larger ship that succeeded the Curlew. Both women were acclaimed for their ability with sword and marlinspike and were often first to board a prize.

In October 1720, Calico Jack's crew successfully captured a merchantman and took to drinking much of the liquid booty in celebration. To the dismay of the two women pirates, the men of the crew were too intoxicated to fight when attacked by a privateer sloop. It was commanded by Captain Barnet, a former pirate turned pirate hunter. Anne Bonny and Mary Read fought against the attackers while Calico Jack and the men huddled beneath the deck of the Revenge, too drunk to fight themselves. Anne became so incensed that she fired her pistol at the men below and screamed, "If there's a man among ye, ye'll come out and fight like the men you are thought to be." Despite their fury and courage, the women and crew were captured.

The women confessed their sex and pleaded to be tried separately from Calico Jack and the men. Both women were pregnant. During a time when women had no legal rights, it was against the law for the state to execute a pregnant woman; no court had the power to condemn an unborn child, no matter how guilty the mother.

Calico Jack was tried on November 16, 1720 and was sentenced to hang. Anne Bonny was given one last visit with him and she cried out to him, "I am sorry to see you here, Jack, but if you'd have fought like a man you needn't hang like a dog." Calico Jack was hung in a gibbet near Port Royal now referred to as Rackham's Cay.

Neither woman was hung. Mary Read died of "white fever" after giving birth in prison. Ironically, her husband, also a member also of Calico Jack's crew, was pardoned. When Anne Bonny's child was born, Anne used her charms to gain two more reprieves. Many suspect her father paid for her freedom. She is alleged to have returned to South Carolina and married yet another pirate, Robert Fenwick, who lived at Fenwick's Castle near Charleston.

3

The Legend of Gasparilla

Webster's Dictionary defines a LEGEND as "a story handed down for generations among a people and popularly believed to have a historical basis, although not verifiable". The story of Jose Gaspar, a.k.a. Gasparilla, Southwest Florida's most famous pirate, is a perfect fit for this definition.

We will share our short mythical version of this legendary pirate in this chapter. In the next chapter we will give you the factual background so you can decide for yourself. And just as the pirate's valued democracy, if you don't like either the legend or the facts, you may create your own version of this myth.

There are multiple and conflicting accounts of this man named Gasparilla. What is unique about his legend is that all accounts follow the same basic timeframe and generally the same events in the life of the pirate who did not exist.

So, for those of you who have not read our historical fiction novels of Gasparilla, we will now narrate our mythical version.

Jose Gaspar was born in 1756 to Ramon and Dulcie Gaspar in the port city of Seville, Spain. As a youngster, though small in stature, Jose proved to be of supreme intelligence and skilled in the use of weapons, often exhibiting leadership among his classmates. At the age of twelve, Jose's involvement with a young girl forced him to leave town to attend the Royal Spanish Naval Academy in Cadiz. Jose Gaspar loved women, and even while at the academy, he had affairs with many ladies, including the commandant's niece.

After graduation, Jose embarked on a naval career in the Spanish Navy. On his first mission, against the Muslim Barbary Pirates, young Jose freed both the crew and a ship being held for ransom in Tripoli. He was quickly promoted to cap-

9

tain's rank and joined the Atlantic Fleet, successfully battling and capturing many Caribbean pirates. His exploits earned him the title of Admiral of the Atlantic Fleet in 1782. In Madrid, the capital, Jose was lionized by his people and became a hero to the Spanish citizens. Because of his great popularity, Jose was called back to Madrid to become the naval attaché in the court of King Charles III.

Admiral Gaspar, a cultured and gallant hero, continued to follow his pattern of seducing women, including the King's daughter-in-law, Maria Luisa, who fell madly in love with him. However, at nearly the same time, Jose met the true love of his life, Dona Rosalita, a beautiful lady of the court. Their marriage was a gala ceremony that became a national event. Jose and Rosalita lived in wedded bliss in a palace outside the capital city where they soon became the proud parents of a son and daughter.

Jose was fearlessly honest and outspoken in his criticism of the corrupt bureaucracy that permeated the Spanish government at the time. This made him the political archenemy of the Prime Minister, Manual Godoy.

Godoy and the jilted Maria Luisa conspired together to destroy Gaspar's career. While he was in command of a convoy transporting the crown jewels, they sent a band of men disguised as robbers to steal the valuables. Though Jose fought valiantly to escape the trap, the jewels were now gone and he was falsely accused by Maria Luisa and Godoy of stealing them himself. Jose managed to return to his home, but, upon his arrival, he was forced to witness Godoy's drunken men terrorizing his family. They viciously murdered his young daughter and his mother-in-law, and raped and murdered his beautiful Dona Rosalita. Waiting until nightfall, Jose took advantage of the drunken state of Godoy's men and killed all those responsible for his wife's death. He then left Madrid with his baby son, whom he left with a trusted friend.

Before leaving his homeland as a wanted criminal, Jose freed men from the king's jail and took possession of a new Spanish warship, the Florida Blanca, which he renamed the Dona Rosalita. The year was 1783, and for the next 38 years, using the alias, Gasparilla, a name that he gave himself, Jose vented his fury against Spain to become the scourge of the high seas.

As time passed, Gasparilla needed to protect his pirate enterprise and abandoned the traditional ports of call in the Caribbean, instead setting up his stronghold on Gasparilla Island in Charlotte Harbor.

Jose, both a freedom-loving gentleman on one hand and a vengeful killer on the other, became a controversial pirate. The circumstances of his mythical life and its psychological impact, have led many writers to devise their own versions of his 38 years as a pirate, based upon their own perception and interpretations. Like most good storytelling, such has been the case in the legend of Gasparilla.

Some say that Gasparilla was brutal, murdering the men whom his pirates captured and holding women hostage for his own and his pirates' pleasure. It is clear that Gasparilla profited from keeping many captives for ransom. It is also believed that Captiva Island was the location where female captives were held until ransom was paid.

There is a recurring story of Gasparilla's capture of a beautiful Spanish princess and his love for her. She completely rejected him despite all his genuine efforts to win her heart. At last, the rejected Gasparilla drew his sword in a fit of anger and cut off the lady's head. In great sorrow, he then buried her headless body on the present day island of Useppa Island. Her head had flown into the Gulf of Mexico and there are those who claim to have seen the headless ghost of this princess in the Charlotte Harbor area.

The final chapter in the Jose Gaspar legend allegedly happened in November 1821, as Jose and his men were preparing to leave Gasparilla Island and move their enterprise to South America. They were leaving Florida because the United States had purchased Florida and were committed to removing all pirates from the coast. A U.S. Navy anti-pirate fleet was operating out of Key West.

As Jose's pirates were preparing to leave Florida, a slow-moving British Merchant vessel was spotted off shore. Jose and his men could not resist temptation and set out for one last adventure.

The "merchant" vessel was actually a United States Navy frigate (often called the USS Enterprise in the legend but, impossible since the ship was actually operating in the Atlantic Ocean at the time.) A fierce battle ensued; but, out manned and outgunned, the Dona Rosalita was critically damaged and began to sink.

Gasparilla, determined not to be captured, leapt to the bow of his stricken ship and shouted to the Americans, "Gasparilla dies by his own hand and not the enemy's." In this author's version, he recognized that his own son was the Captain of the U.S. Navy ship, wrapped himself in his pirate flag (an anchor chain described in most legends is actually too heavy to lift) and dived into the Gulf of Mexico.

This enduring story has been retold and rewritten many times to become the Legend of Jose Gaspar or Gasparilla, Southwest Florida's historical pirate king.

In the next chapter, you will learn the historical basis for how this larger-than-life character became a legend. And, in future chapters, we will continue to share some local pirate stories from Southwest Florida, including proven details so that you, the reader, can decide for yourself, is it legend or is it fact? Or, as is often the case, what is it we choose to believe.

4

The FACTS About The Gasparilla Legend

We discussed the legendary pirate Jose Gaspar, or Gasparilla, in our last segment. We maintain that the story of Gasparilla is a myth, as there are no historical facts that would indicate that he ever existed, particularly as described in the local lore and legends. However, it appears that pirates used this name during various sackings along the Mexico and Cuban coasts. There is even a monument in the city of Campeche, Mexico, which allegedly honors the citizens who battled and defended their city from an annual sacking by a pirate named Jose Gaspar from an island off Florida.

But, the historical facts that follow regrettably indicate that Jose Gaspar, or Gasparilla, our most famous local legend, simply never existed.

1. With the exception of Lover's Key, that did derive its name from the pirates Anne Bonny and Calico Jack Rackham, all the islands along our coast were named and on navigational maps long before Gasparilla and his pirates allegedly arrived. Mound Key is a man made island built for safety against the natural elements and security from possible invaders. (1) Mound Key was built about the time of the pyramids in Egypt by the Caloosa (also spelled Calusa) Indians. These first developers of Florida built this island and others thousands of years before the time of Gasparilla. The island named Sanibel, a corrupted version of "Spanish," first appeared on a map dating from 1765 during the period that the English controlled Florida. Fishing ranchos, populated by Cuban Spanish fisherman, dotted all the coastal islands from the 1600's until 1900. (2) These islands were all known by the names we know today and include Gasparilla Island, Cayo Costa, Pine Island, Sanibel, Estero, and Captiva islands. Gasparilla Island actually got its name from a Spanish Catholic missionary, named either Gaspar or Gasparillo who estab-

lished a mission on the island bearing his name to minister to these Spanish fishermen and even the Calusas that traded with them. (3)

2. The Spanish were known for their meticulous record keeping. There is no record of Jose Gaspar's service in their navy during the period he was alleged to have quickly risen to the rank of Admiral. In fact, nowhere, in either Spanish or American history, is there any information that would indicate Gaspar ever existed. (4)

3. During the alleged years of Gasparilla's reign in Southwest Florida, 1783-1821, there was, in fact, no pirate activity reported on Florida's west coast. During the period between the American Revolution and the War of 1812, there was virtually no sea going traffic among the harbors in the Gulf of Mexico. Most piracy during this period occurred on the northern coast of Cuba and the eastern coast of Florida. (3)

4. The person who gets most of the credit for telling and retelling the basic Gasparilla pirate story was John Gomez, also called Juan Gomez, who claimed to be an eyewitness and, at times, to have been a pirate in the pirate confederation of Jose Gaspar. Gomez, a hermit, lived on Pavilion Key in a hut. There are many versions of his life as well. Gomez was born in 1778. He claimed to have been a sailor on board a ship Gaspar captured, becoming a pirate and serving with Gaspar through his demise. Juan Gomez accidentally drowned around 1900 at the age of 122 years, according to some sources. (4)

5. The first written version of the Gasparilla legend came in an advertising brochure of the Charlotte Harbor and Northern Railroad Company operated by Henry B. Plant. This brochure, printed around 1900, was given to customers of the railroad and the Boca Grande Hotel. It is obvious that this brochure relied heavily upon the stories told by John or Juan Gomez who died that year. (4)

6. In 1902, after Plant's death three years earlier, the Plant Railroad Empire was sold. The offices were moved from Charlotte Harbor to Tampa along with the Legend of Gasparilla story. The business people of Tampa, originally wanting to promote a "Mardi Gras" type of event for the city, were inspired enough to promote the first Gasparilla Pirate Days celebration in 1904. Today it has become one of the most popular month long festivals in

the world. One of the ironies is that Southwest Florida's Pine Island was named "Tampa" on early navigational maps.

7. Various early 20th century historians were taken in by the business interests promoting the Gasparilla festival in Tampa and reported the existence of Jose Gaspar or Gasparilla as historical fact. (4)

The importance of noting the facts in this chapter is that many of the pirates we will be discussing in the future chapters are often times tied to the mythical Gasparilla of Charlotte Harbor, either in outright legend or alleged "fact."

---

1. Schell, Rolfe F., *1,000 Years on Mound Key*, Island Press, Ft. Myers, Fl., 1962, pg. 14

2. Anholt, Betty, *Sanibel's Story, Voices and Images*, The Donnelly Co. Publishers, 1998, pg. 11

3. Bickel, Karl A., *The Mangrove Coast: The Story of the West Coast of Florida*, Coward-McCann, New York, 1942, pg. 108-117.

4. Ans, Andre-Marcel d', *The Legend of Gasparilla: Myth and History on Florida's West Coast*, Tampa Bay History, 1980.

5

Brewster Baker, Legendary Pirate, a Legendary Name

Brewster Baker allegedly was one of the most successful of the little-known pirates who operated in the waters around Florida. The name, Brewster Baker, has also been used as a fictional name for an outlaw in the Wild West and is also a name used in many B cowboy movies in the 1940's and 1950's. In addition, Brewster Baker is the name of the main character, played by Kenny Rodgers, in the 1982 comedy/drama movie, Six Pack, a film that featured NASCAR stock car racing in its early years. So, the name Brewster Baker is indeed legendary.

Brewster Baker, the Southwest Florida pirate, is said to have been a British naval officer in the late 1700's. In 1797, while serving as a lieutenant aboard the British frigate HMS Heather, off the coast of Barbados, he was the leader of a successful mutiny. Baker and the seamen loyal to him put the remaining crew ashore and were thus forced to become pirates. The first ship that they captured off the French island of Guadeloupe was the Andre Follet, a French ship of adequate size and speed that became their flagship. To avoid capture, Baker and his men sailed into the Gulf of Mexico and sought refuge on one of the many islands dotting the "Mangrove Coast."

British navy regulations of the late 1700's required that any naval ship operating in the waters around Florida could not cross over the mean high tide line when in pursuit of any combatant or pirate. This was primarily a safety issue as the waters in the Gulf of Mexico are often very shallow and a ship run aground is liable to sink or suffer attack from its original prey.

As a former British officer, Brewster Baker both knew and used to his advantage the rules that the British navy operated under. Baker would often enter San Carlos Bay or the mouth of the Caloosahatchee River, knowing that the British would cease chasing his ship once it was safely on the landside of the mean high tide line.

The barrier islands along the Southwest Florida coast allowed Brew Baker, as he began calling himself, many avenues of escape from any national navy pursuer. One of Baker's favorite ploys was to sail his ship up Long Cut at the south end of present day Pine Island. He would then have rigging attached to his tall masts. After going ashore, some of his crew would pull the ship over and tie the top of the masts to the dense mangrove trees. From the water, the masts could not be seen and the dense mangroves provided camouflage so that pursuers could not find his ship. Long Cut became known as "Bru Baker's Cut" among the fishermen around Pine Island and was also noted as such on many maps.

In 1798, Brew Baker and his men sailed up Pine Island Sound and established a pirate community on the small island of Bojelia just off the northern tip of Pine Island. The English sailors soon were pronouncing this name "Bokeelia". Because of the shallow waters surrounding Bokeelia, large vessels could not access it. This gave Baker a great defensive advantage with his limited crew of men. The island had a fresh water supply and fertile soil. Fish were plentiful in the area and the sandy beaches provided an excellent area to career their ships. Baker and his men established a village of palmetto-thatched huts and established a community that traded with both the Indians and the Spanish Fishing Ranchos in the area. From this community, Baker and his pirate crew would sail to plunder the North Coast of Cuba as well as the shipping lanes from Latin America through the Florida Keys.

Baker, who in later years was known as Brew Baker, Bru Baker, and Brubaker allegedly worked with the legendary Jose Gaspar in Charlotte Harbor as well as the Lafitte brothers who were operating out of New Orleans at the time. The alleged association with the Lafitte brothers has some historical merit while we question the existence of Jose Gaspar.

But, by 1820, Florida had become a United States territory and twenty-seven American ships had been attacked and plundered off the coast of Florida by pirates like Baker. The insurance companies and politicians demanded effective action be taken against pirates operating around Florida. In 1821, President James Monroe authorized the United States Navy to establish an anti-pirate squadron in order to rid Caribbean of piracy. David Porter was appointed to command this unit that included the first steamship used by the United States Navy.

With the American navy threatening his settlement on Bokeelia, Brew Baker and his crew sailed from Charlotte Harbor intent on resettling in South America. Enroute, Captain Baker went ashore in the Gulf of Darien and was attacked by native Indians. He suffered a poisoned arrow to the chest and died an agonizing death.

6

John Gomez, A Living Legend Who Created Legends

John Gomez, or Juan Gomez, was himself a living legend of Southwest Florida. Gomez actually lived in Southwest Florida and became a larger than life character in his own right. He is the also the source for much of the local pirate lore that has been attributed to this area, including alleged characters and events. What made his stories believable was the fact that he, as in the case of the Gasparilla story, always subordinated himself and his role in the tales that he often told anxious audiences.

So, who was John or Juan Gomez? Gomez claimed to have been born on the Portuguese island of Madeira in 1778. At the age of 12, his family moved to Lisbon. Juan Gomez did not approve of the move and immediately ran away from home. He traveled to France and three years later, at 15 years of age, joined the French navy as a cabin boy. When his ship reached the West Indies, Gomez deserted the French navy and joined the crew of a Spanish merchant vessel, the Villa Rica, one of the last of the famous Spanish galleons.

During his tenure as a sailor on the Villa Rica, Gomez traveled the world. According to his story, his ship was blown far off course in 1801 by a late September hurricane. It was captured, looted, and burned off the Southwest Florida coast by a pirate called Gasparilla. Gomez later told the story that all the crew of the doomed ship, except for himself, were knifed and killed by the pirates. He claimed that Gasparilla personally intervened to save his life and that of eleven young Mexican women. Gomez then described how Gasparilla assigned the young women to members of his pirate crew, except for one who was alleged to have been the daughter of a Mexican Viceroy. Gomez said that Gasparilla fell in

19

love with this girl, Josefa, but later he beheaded her in a fit of rage. This began the tale of Gasparilla, the pirate king of Boca Grande.

Juan Gomez alleged that he then went to Spain, under orders from Gasparilla, to assassinate Manual Godoy, the Prime Minister of Spain. He never reached Godoy, but instead joined the French Army's Black Dragoons where he claimed to have been spoken to by Napoleon Bonaparte. According to Gomez, Napoleon patted him on the shoulder and said to him, "You will make a fine soldier some-day." The complex Gomez then said that he deserted his post and joined a ship bound for Charleston, South Carolina.

Gomez spent the next ten years as a member of the crew of a slave ship. He didn't talk much about this part of his life. However, Gomez stated that in 1818 he was again captured by the pirate Gasparilla and spent the next three years on Boca Grande as a member of the pirate confederation. Gomez claimed to have wit-nessed from shore the demise of Gasparilla at the hands of the American navy pirate hunters. He and the other pirates left on shore took a small boat, sailed down Pine Island Sound, and took refuge on Panther Key.

Gomez eventually boarded a schooner sailing to Havana, Cuba, and resumed his career as a crewman on a slave ship. It should be noted that slavery was a lucrative business and those who participated in this trade were often well rewarded finan-cially, compared to the wages of merchant seaman or naval sailors.

In 1831, Gomez was involved in a revolt against Spanish authorities in Cuba and was forced to flee to St. Augustine. Since the Golden Age of Piracy was over and the last remaining traditional pirates were gone, he remained in St. Augustine until he was hired as a scout for General Zachary Taylor's command during the Seminole War. Gomez was 59 years old when he fought in the Battle of Lake Okeechobee on Christmas Day of 1837. The following year he was discharged from service and moved to Cedar Key on the Gulf Coast to become a "cracker" or a Florida cowboy. He remained there until 1855.

At 77 years of age, Gomez returned to Panther Key and built a palmetto shack. With the onset of the Civil War, he returned to the sea and, by his own words, became involved in blockade running, which paid him handsomely. Gomez was then 87 years old but still possessed great physical prowess. He often challenged younger men to physical contests such as climbing trees, and regularly climbed coconut palms after milk nuts, as he called them.

Gomez became a friend of Walter T. Collier and his son, William D. Collier. They constituted the first family to live on what is now Marco Island in 1870 and operated a general store. The Colliers were impressed by John Gomez and regaled in the stories the old man told them.

In 1884, 106-year-old John Gomez arrived back on Panther Key with his new bride. The well-educated 78-year-old lady had married him in Tampa. The couple then fell on hard times and became destitute.

Friends of Gomez, led by Captain Collier, traveled to Fort Myers and requested that the Commissioners of the newly-formed Lee County pay Collier's store the sum of $ 8.00 per month to provide food and clothing to the destitute couple living on Panther Key. These payments may have constituted the first welfare payments made by Lee County.

When news of the old ex-pirate living on Panther Key among the Ten Thousand Islands of Florida's Southwest Coast spread, it brought many a sailor, yachtsman and treasure hunter to the area. They yearned to meet Gomez and listen to his many stories of pirates, his years in the slave trade, or his military adventures. John Gomez made a considerable amount of money by dispensing his incredible stories to those willing to believe them and by telling where treasures were allegedly buried. The stories were believable since he always cast himself as a minor player or someone who knew something others did not.

One hot July day in 1900, the legendary old man, at age 122, went fishing in his beloved Gulf of Mexico. It was to be the old pirate's last voyage. Gomez apparently became entangled in the draw cord of his casting net and was thrown overboard. He drowned in the clear blue water.

Beater, Jack, *Pirates and Buried Treasure on Florida Islands*, St. Petersburg: Great Outdoors Publishing Co., 1959, pgs. 17—22.

Grismer, Karl H., The *Story of Fort Myers*, A Southwest Florida Historical Society Book, Fort Myers Beach: The Island Publishers, 1982, pages 45 & 46.

Ans, Andre-Marcel d', *The Legend of Gasparilla: Myth and History on Florida's West Coast*, Tampa Bay History, 1980.

Burnett, Gene M., *Florida's Past: People & Events That Shaped The State Volume 2*, Sarasota, FL, Pineapple Press, 1988, pages 95-99.

7

Lafitte's Treasures and Other Treasure Legends of Southwest Florida

As we discussed in previous chapters, in almost every area claiming to have had pirates, there are also stories of pirate treasures of gold and silver or hidden chests of pirate booty. One of the most famous of these legends, which includes the area of Southwest Florida, is that of Jean Lafitte's hidden treasure. Jean Lafitte himself contributed to these tales, often boasting that he personally supervised the hiding places of millions of dollars of valuables. He once stated that, across the Gulf of Mexico, near Galveston, he had buried enough money to build a solid-gold bridge across the Mississippi River. The fact is that Lafitte, although not a seaman himself, employed thousands of sailors and many ships to raid and plunder shipping throughout the Caribbean. Many of these sailors and ships made port in the deep-water harbors of Charlotte and Tampa Bay, which makes claims of Lafitte's treasure a possibility.

Lafitte's treasure was alleged to have been buried in every inlet and upon every island along the entire coast of the Gulf of Mexico. Jean Lafitte and his brother were said to have buried millions of dollars both in San Carlos Bay and up the Peace River in Charlotte Harbor. The problem with these stories is that Jean Lafitte, historically called "The Pirate of the Gulf", went to sea only ONCE in his life when he sailed from France to New Orleans in 1809. Lafitte seems to have taken credit for almost all pirate activity that took place along the Gulf of Mexico during the time that he lived there. That is why he is one of history's most romantic and enigmatic characters. Lord Byron is quoted as saying; "He left a corsair's name to other times, Linked one virtue to a thousand crimes."

Another problem, and one with environmental concerns, is that, based upon these and other treasure stories, many of our beaches, islands, rivers, and inlets have been dug up at one time or another with no treasures ever being found. Although there have been coins, pieces of silver and other items discovered, these discoveries should not be considered a valuable treasure trove. There is even some evidence that items may have been "planted" by those who would profit from visitors who would come to search for buried treasure. The real tragedy is that normally rational people have dug up Indian mounds, graves, and historical sites, actually destroying archeological sites, while looking for Lafitte's and others' supposedly buried treasure.

Jean Lafitte was handsome and was conversant in French, Spanish, Italian and English. He was a polished gentleman and a shrewd businessman who amassed a fortune by smuggling slaves and merchandise past the local customs inspectors. Lafitte operated his enterprise from his roost on Grand Terre Island, a commune that included a café, bordello, gambling den, warehouses, a barracoon (for detaining slaves), and outdoor bazaars that offered silks, spices, wines, and furniture. Grand Terre Island was located in the huge wetlands of Barataria Bay near New Orleans. From this fortified outpost, Jean Lafitte controlled the entire import traffic of the lower Mississippi River. He also had control over most of the shipping throughout the Gulf of Mexico and Southwest Florida during this period of his operations.

Lafitte was both cruel and generous, a patriot and pirate. The many stories of Lafitte had him making deals with men as well as the devil. A French legend tells of Jean Lafitte striking a bargain with the Devil. According to this legend, Lafitte's castle on Galveston Island, where he moved after the War of 1812, was called Maison Rouge (Red House), and was built by the Devil himself in a single night. Lafitte, in exchange for Maison Rouge, offered the Devil the life and soul of the first creature that Lafitte would cast his eyes upon the next morning. Without the Devil's knowledge, Lafitte then arranged to have a dog thrown into his tent at daybreak, so that all the Devil got out of the deal was a dog.

There are few characters in history to compare with Jean Lafitte. Andrew Jackson, the American hero of the War of 1812, and later president of the United States, condemned, exonerated and again condemned Lafitte's actions. When he sought Jean Lafitte's help in fighting the British, Lafitte, always the negotiator, agreed to fight for the Americans if Jackson were to promise clemency and grant citizenship to his privateers, the Baratarians. Jackson consented, and most historians agree that were it not for Lafitte's powder, flints, and extraordinary bombarding by Dominique You (Lafitte's brother) Great Britain would have won the Battle of New Orleans that foggy morning of January 8, 1815. Later, Lafitte was forced to leave and move to Galveston Island, where he built Maison Rouge. He was embittered that America again had rejected him and died a broken man on May 11, 1821.

Jean Lafitte will always be remembered for two reasons. One is that during the War of 1812, on the field at Chalmette, near New Orleans, for a few glorious hours he was a proud American and true American hero. Unfortunately, the second reason is that in our archeological history he has become known as the man who claimed to have buried gold and other treasures in every inlet and upon every island along the entire Gulf Coast.

Other legendary treasures allegedly buried in Southwest Florida include the following sites and information:

- Calico Jack Rackham allegedly buried over $ 3,000,000.00 somewhere in the Ten Thousand Islands.

- 14 tons of silver was buried on the coast of Sanibel Island that had been plundered by "Black Caesar".

- The non-existent pirate Jose Gaspar or Gasparilla on Gasparilla Island buried over $ 2,000,000.00 in gold and silver.

- Indian gold and silver worth millions, stolen from the Spanish or recovered from shipwrecks, is allegedly buried inland from Mound Key, to the north of Tampa Bay.

Legends of sunken treasure ships around Florida still persist to this day in spite of modern sophisticated electronics, the many military maneuvers and activities of both the air force and the navy, the existence of companies that actually do hunt buried and sunken treasures, and the fact that Florida waters are among the most dived waters in the world. Remember that, as we have discussed throughout this chapter, if the treasures were actually there they would probably have been discovered by now. So, each of the following is more legend than actual fact:

- 1529—A Spanish ship wrecked at Punta Rassa. The ship was a Hernando de Soto supply ship that was caught in a storm and sank at the mouth of the Caloosahatchee River. The cargo was alleged to have been the payroll and armament and supplies for De Soto's Expedition.

- 1563—A galleon of the 1563 Vera Cruz fleet wrecked in the shallows of Charlotte Harbor with an unknown value of treasure aboard.

- 1600—An unnamed 200-ton nao, built in France and coming from Mexico, under the command of Captain Diego Rodriquez, sank off the west coast of Florida near the Ten Thousand Islands.

- 1641—A Spanish galleon, San Cristoforo, was caught in a hurricane and sunk in shallow water off north end of Sanibel Island. The cargo was reported to contain over a million dollars in gold bars and coins.

- 1733—A Spanish galleon wrecked at Clam Pass. The ship was part of a Spanish fleet sailing from Mexico to Cuba. A hurricane scattered wreckage along the shoreline of Clam Pass where gold coins were found on the beach.

- 1733—A Spanish galleon, sister ship to the wreck found at Clam Pass was sunk by a hurricane. It had a cargo of over one million dollars in gold coins that were never recovered.

- 1733—A Spanish galleon, either a part of a fleet caught in a hurricane or sunk later by pirates. was sunk at the mouth of Caxambas Pass south of Marco Island. Treasure cargo unknown.

- 1803—A pirate ship was sunk by a British warship about one half mile offshore from Black Island. The pirates were captured and hung. The cargo was never recovered.

- 1817-An unidentified wreck was discovered at Bocilla Pass. It was believed to have been sunk by pirates in the area. Cannon and ballast were recovered from this site. The cargo was unknown.

- 1817—A pirate ship was sunk by British ships off La Costa Island. It was believed to be part of Lafitte's fleet of privateers. The crew was captured and hung under British Admiralty Law.

- 1821—The ship, Florida Blanca, allegedly Gasparilla the pirate's flagship and treasure vessel, was sunk by the American navy with a treasure on board of 9 million dollars. This obviously never occurred!

- 1821—An American frigate lies at the Gulf entrance to Big Gasparilla Pass. The ship was carrying over one million dollars in coin bound for New Orleans.

- 1863—A Confederate Ship, the Queen Mary, was sunk by the Union Navy warship, Hatteras, offshore from Captiva Island at Redfish Pass. The Queen Mary was carrying guns, ammunition, and payroll money to Tampa for overland shipment to the Confederate army.

Since the Civil War, there have been many more ships and barges sunk in the waters off the coast of Southwest Florida. Many of these were yachts and ships belonging to some of the richest men on earth and are rumored to carry valuables. There is even the story of Battista's Gold. Allegedly a B-25 belonging to Cuba's deposed Dictator and carrying 25 million dollars in gold crashed into the Gulf of Mexico off the Southwest Florida coast during the Cuban Revolution that saw Fidel Castro seize power.

> However, if you are considering organizing a treasure hunt, it might be wise to simply invest in a metal detector and settle for some of the modern coins and jewelry that you might find on our busy tourist beaches.

> Or, if you want to seek historical finds in Southwest Florida, invest in a spaghetti colander and a diving mask and look for MEGALODON shark teeth. From Boca Grande north to Venice Beach and the inland waters, these 7 to 10 million old shark's teeth are found on a regular basis. There is no doubt these teeth have a true history, unlike the treasures described in this story.

> Some studies indicate that there is more gold underwater in the world's oceans than we have available on land today. Unfortunately, Southwest Florida and our part of the Gulf of Mexico is not the repository of this gold, or any other buried or sunken treasures. Enjoy the legends, but always respect our environment.

American Folklore and Legend, Pleasantville, NY, The Reader's Digest Association, 1978, pages 80-81.

Handbook of Texas Online, s.v.".," http://www.tsha.utexas.edu/handbook/online/articles/LL/fla12.html (accessed March 13, 2007).

The Story of Jean and Pierre Lafitte, the Pirate-Patriots, New Orleans: Louisiana State Museum/Press of T. J. Moran;s Sons, 1938.

8

Blockade Runners and the Development of Southwest Florida during the Civil War

We have learned that piracy is about freedom, power, and financial gain. We have also learned that what constitutes a pirate to one nation, may be referred to as a "privateer" by another employing nation. We will learn in this chapter that forms of piracy will always be a part of our history, present and future.

During the American Civil War, "privateers" served the Confederate States of America in Southwest Florida by loading shiploads of cattle and needed supplies at ports along the west coast of Florida. They then sailed with these supplies to the Southern States. Few people realize that during that time, a second Civil War took place within the State of Florida. In fact, Fort Myers, the county seat of Lee County, actually was born as a result of this Florida Civil War.

At the time of its formation, no one could have envisioned that the North's East Gulf Coast Blockading Squadron would be instrumental in creating a civil war within the State of Florida or that, with its allies, the refugees and contrabands (escaped slaves); it would be one of the more active foes of the Confederacy in Florida. (1) Abraham Lincoln's naval blockade began April 19, 1861. From this point on, the privateers serving the Confederacy became known as "Blockade Runners."

Although Fort Pickens in Pensacola, Fort Jefferson in the Dry Tortugas, and Fort Taylor at Key West remained Union forts throughout the Civil War, the "blockade runners" were initially successful in supplying the confederacy. These privateers took needed supplies to the Confederates and brought cotton and tobacco crops on the return voyages, making sizeable profits for the crews and owners of these ships.

However; the East Coast Blockading Squadron took advantage of three factors to begin a civil war within Florida: 1. There was a limited non-native population in Southwest Florida, due to the fact that the Third Seminole War had just ended in 1858 and much of the military action during that war took place on the Peace, Kissimmee, and Caloosahatchee rivers and the Big Cypress Swamp meaning the area around Charlotte Harbor had been open to white settlement for only three years before the war; 2. Forts that had been built during the Third Seminole War, although abandoned, were still in existence and could be used to house troops and refugees; 3. Southwest Florida's limited non-Indian population was composed primarily of refugees from the Civil War, deserters from the Confederacy, and contrabands (former black slaves), which meant that this unique population opposed to the ideals of the Confederate states became an important source of manpower for the Union navy.

To inspire and lead this unique group of refugees and contrabands to fight for the union cause, the Union navy chose Henry A. Crane, a printer and former Florida military officer during the Seminole War. He was living in Tampa and became a refugee himself from the Confederacy. It is ironic that Crane who, in the opening days of the Civil War, had actually formed the Silver Grays, a group of older military men living in Tampa, for "the purpose of home defense." Henry Crane refused a commission as lieutenant colonel in the Confederate Army and left his wife and daughters in Tampa to fight for the Union. His only son joined the Confederate army making his family a house divided which was common during the American Civil War.

Crane, who had led inland military action on the east coast of Florida to harass the rebels and destroy Confederate property, came to Southwest Florida and was stationed aboard the *USS Rosalie* in Charlotte Harbor. Henry Crane also brought a number of refugee families who were Union sympathizers to Charlotte Harbor to settle on Useppa Island under the protection of the Union navy. These refugees of Useppa Island provided valuable information to the Union navy and also became pilots, guides, and even fighters for the Union cause. Since the refugees were from Florida, they provided information to the Union navy on the identity of the Southern privateers and blockade-runners. Often the blockade-runners were fellow Floridians from the same local communities.

Henry Crane established the first post of refugee soldiers at Fort Myers. On January 3, 1864, Crane led two boats from Punta Rassa up the Caloosahatchee River to the deserted former army post, Fort Myers, that had been built before the Third Seminole War. General Woodbury, Henry Crane's commander, along with members of the Forty-seventh Pennsylvania Volunteers came to Fort Myers to recruit refugees and former black slaves to man and defend Fort Myers. Woodbury also moved his military base for operations from Useppa Island to Fort Myers because Useppa Island was too dependent on water transportation to operate at maximum advantage.

Henry Crane was named commander of Fort Myers and was transferred from the Union navy to the United States Army as a Captain. Crane and his 170 former black slaves known as the Second Infantry Regiment, U.S. Colored Troops, served the Union well and gave notice to the citizens of Southwest Florida that the union army was here to stay. These troops raided and harassed cattle shipments and caused significant disruption in the area so that it limited any future successes of the blockade-runners for the remainder of the Civil War.

Fort Myers remained until after the end of the Civil War. When it was closed after the war, many of the people remained and Fort Myers is today is a vibrant city, thanks to an intrastate civil war to control and defeat the supply sources of the privateers who were the blockade-runners for the Confederacy.

In the decades since the Civil War, the 1,380 miles of coastline that surrounds all Florida have seen pirates, privateers, crime syndicates, and independents become smugglers of nearly every commodity known to man. Generally this activity has occurred when the Federal or State government has enacted laws that are not supported by the population as a whole

---

Buker, George E., *"Blockaders, refugees, and contrabands: civil war on Florida's Gulf Coast, 1861-1865,"* Tuscaloosa, Alabama: The University of Alabama Press, 1993.

Burnett, Gene M., "Florida's Past, People & Events That Shaped the State," Pineapple Press, Sarasota, Florida, 1988, pages 84-87.

"Despite embargo, U.S. top food source for island," *The News-Press (Ft. Myers, FL) (March 26, 2007),* page A7

9

From Civil War Through Prohibition

In the decades since the Civil War, the 1,380 miles of irregular coastline that borders Florida have seen pirates, privateers, crime syndicates, and independents become smugglers of nearly every commodity known to man. As we have read, the 17th and 18th century pirates took full advantage of the shallow waters, mangrove islands, inlets, and even swamps of Southwest Florida to carry on a variety of illegal pursuits. In the years following the Civil War, not only liquors, and drugs, and other commodities were smuggled into Southwest Florida; the smuggling of human beings also became a profitable enterprise and remains so today.

Often, this illegal activity has occurred when the Federal or State government has enacted laws that are not supported by the population as a whole. The greatest example of such a law was the 18th Amendment, begun in 1920 as the "noble experiment." This amendment, called Prohibition, became one of most colorful, sordid, and ignoble chapters in Florida's history. Prohibition led to the development of the Florida rumrunners. Although initially more active on Florida's East Coast during this period, schooners, motorboats, and freighters soon began using Southwest Florida as a drop off point for Cuban rum or British Scotch from the Bahamas. Like the drug smuggling and human trafficking that followed, this could be a very profitable venture. For example, a rumrunner could legally buy a case of Cuban rum in Cuba for $ 4.00 per case and sell it in Florida for over $ 100.00. The Southwest Florida coastline with its mangrove-fringed Ten Thousand Islands, shallow waters with navigable cuts and deep harbors remains a smuggler's dream to this day.

Although smugglers had to worry about the United States Coast Guard, they also had to worry about other smugglers or pirates waiting to steal their cargo either at sea or on delivery on the shore. Stealing illegal liquor, guns and money was easy money during the turbulent times of Prohibition.

Many terms we use in our daily conversations have their roots in piracy, smuggling, rum running, and other illegal pursuits.

The term "belling the cat" became popular during this period. Large freighters or mother ships would remain legally offshore with their cargo and smaller boats or runners would off-load the cargo and race it to shore. If the coast guard were patrolling in the area, the first runner boat would go through the motions of off-loading the mother ship and lead the coast guard vessel in pursuit. Typically, the coast guard would successfully stop the first boat, only to be shown empty boxes or no cargo at all. While the coast guard pursued the first runner, another runner went to the mother ship, off-loaded the real cargo, and took it to shore by another route.

Captain Bill McCoy was originally from Jacksonville, Florida. He was a skilled boat builder who turned to smuggling rum after the enactment of Prohibition. He founded Rum Row, which was a chain of mother ships along America's east coast from New England to the tip of Florida, which provided rumrunners the illegal alcohol for smuggling ashore in smaller boats. McCoy had associates among Southwest Florida Cuban rumrunners who were known to sell cheap rye from Cuba. These Florida rumrunners agreed to steer customers in search of quality liquors to McCoy because he had a reputation for only selling the finest alcoholic beverages. The term "the real McCoy" is now a part of our everyday language. One odd fact is that Captain McCoy was a self-confessed "teetotaler" who never consumed alcohol.

Two of the most infamous liquor pirates were from Southwest Florida. James Horace Alderman was born June 24, 1883 in Hillsborough County, but moved to the Ten Thousand Islands as a child. In his younger years he became famous as a fishing guide for President Teddy Roosevelt, Zane Grey, and others in their quest for tarpon fishing. These experiences led Horace Alderman to learn the intricacies of the Southwest Florida coast.

Alderman married Pearl Robinson of Lee County on April 8, 1906, in Fort Myers, Florida. After his marriage he ran a poolroom that was a rendezvous for high stake gamblers among the pioneer cattlemen of the Everglades. Before prohibition, Alderman was involved in numerous illegal adventures at sea along the Southwest Florida coastline, most often involving smuggling Chinese and other nationalities from Cuba into Florida at both Punta Rassa in Lee County and Chokoloskee Island in the Ten Thousand Islands in Collier County. He would contract to bring cargoes of aliens into the United States, receive large fees, and then drown the helpless foreigners from his boats. Alderman was accused of killing at least 17 Chinese aliens by throwing them overboard and drowning them between Cuba and Southwest Florida. Legend claims an even larger death toll.

With the passage of the 18th Amendment, much more money could be made in transporting liquor so Alderman went on to become a rumrunner. During his early days of smuggling liquor, Alderman made the mistake of employing a customs agent as a cook on his boat that ran from the Bahamas. He was arrested and convicted, serving one year and one day for this infraction. He then returned to full-scale smuggling of both liquor and aliens until the Coast Guard captured him 35 miles southwest of Miami on August 27, 1927, carrying 50 containers of whiskey. Alderman was taken on board the Coast Guard cutter where he drew his pistol and killed two Coast Guardsmen and a Secret Service man. He briefly took control of the cutter, threatening to burn it and kill all the crew, but was subsequently subdued and taken to the Coast Guard base at Bahia Mar in Fort Lauderdale on the East coast. James Horace Alderman had been declared a pirate in Broward County and was now convicted of murder in Dade County. Since maritime law decreed that a pirate be hanged at the port where lawmen first brought him, James Horace Alderman was hung in a seaplane hanger at Bahia Mar in Fort Lauderdale on August 17, 1929. He is one of only two federal prisoners ever executed in Florida.

The other Southwest Florida rum running smuggler was "Wicked Frank Lowe" who initially was a pirate operating in the Bahamas. Frank Lowe was born near Charlotte Harbor in 1891 and was unique in the fact that; unlike today's smugglers who steal fast boats to ply their trade, Frank Lowe built his own swift boats to outrun the Coast Guard cutters. Like James Alderman, Frank Lowe smuggled both liquor from Cuba as well as Chinese immigrants wanting to get to the freedoms of the United States. And, like James Alderman, Frank Lowe allegedly murdered many of the Chinese immigrants who had paid him to take them to Southwest Florida. In addition, many people believe that Frank Lowe along with some of his fellow smugglers, murdered Collier County Sheriff's Deputy J.H.

Cox and his wife and two children. Frank Lowe definitely lived up to his name of Wicked Frank Lowe.

Any time in our history that unpopular laws like Prohibition are passed; there is the opportunity to make money. The Florida rumrunners were willing to take risks to bring in products that many people wanted. This often gave them an aura of romance and bravado to the people of the United States.

———————————

Burnett, Gene M., *Florida's Past: People & Events That Shaped The State Volume 2*, Sarasota, FL, Pineapple Press, 1988, pages 84-87.

Babson, Jennifer, "Cuban migrant smugglers find new launch spot," *Herald (Miami, FL) (May 16, 2005)*: NA. Junior Edition. Thomson Gale.

Caudle, Hal M., *The Hanging at Bahia Mar*, Fort Lauderdale: Wake-Brook House, 1976.

McCarthy, Kevin M., *Nine Florida Stories by Marjory Stoneman Douglas*, Jacksonville: University of North Florida Press, 1990, pgs 74-96.

"Alderman Held Criminal Record in Fort Myers, At One Time Acted As Fishing Guide for President Roosevelt, Fort Myers Tropical News, Fort Myers, FL, January 28, 1928.

Husty, Denes, "Smugglers have centuries-old history in SW Florida," The News-Press, (August 6, 2007) pages A1, A10

10

From Prohibition Until Today

When the profit was taken from liquor and rum running by the repeal of the 18th Amendment on December 5, 1933, liquor smuggling declined. Prior to World War II, however, it was replaced by gun smuggling from Southwest Florida to Central American countries, with narcotics coming back on the return trip.

During World War II, many German agents were smuggled into South Florida where they blended in with the many American servicemen training at bases throughout Florida. Unlike the human smuggling before and after the war, no Americans participated or profited from these illegals landing off German submarines.

After World War II, the Coast Guard's primary responsibility shifted largely to safety at sea and aiding navigation. This lasted up to the Cuban Revolution in 1959 when the Coast Guard again took on the responsibility of stopping smuggling of men and weapons.

During the period of the late 1960's through the early 1980's, smugglers in Southwest Florida starting hauling marijuana by the ton in bales that were called, "Square Grouper." Collier County became the port of entry for marijuana from all of South America. Like the human smugglers today, marijuana-laden freighters from South America anchored offshore serving as "Mother Ships" to smaller boats often piloted by local fisherman who knew the waters offshore and were able to successfully ferry to shore marijuana in quantities measured in tons! A Federal crackdown in the mid 1980's in Everglades City and Chokoloskee, dubbed Operation Everglades resulted in the seizure of dozens of boats and vehicles and at least $252 million in marijuana, and the sentencing of many local smugglers.

Following marijuana, cocaine became the most smuggled drug into Southwest Florida. Southwest Floridians plying this trade soon became known as "Cocaine Cowboys."

In the early 1970's, drug interception became an increasing emphasis for the Coast Guard. Illegal or non-prescribed drug use has been a problem for societies for almost 7,000 years. Millions of dollars are spent annually to enforce drug laws while members of our society wanting to use these illegal drugs spend billions of dollars. The State of Florida in general and Southwest Florida in particular are primary areas for international drug trafficking and money laundering organizations, as well as a principal thoroughfare for cocaine and heroin transiting to the Northeastern United States and Canada. The increase in the price of shipping drugs through Mexico as well as the increased United States Federal law enforcement efforts on the southwestern borders of the U.S. have brought the Colombian cocaine smugglers back to their traditional routes through the Caribbean and into Florida.

The drugs currently smuggled into Southwest Florida include Crack Cocaine, Methamphetamine, MDMA and other club drugs, as well as "Pharmaceutical Diversion" of prescription drugs through illegal use of the Internet. Marijuana is still imported but domestic indoor cultivation is a significant industry in Southwest Florida with nearly every community having discovered "grow houses" in residential neighborhoods.

Like the rumrunners of the past, cocaine traffickers rely on "go fast" boats to smuggle cocaine. These "go fast" boats are custom fiberglass boats that can travel 50 mph with their 800 horsepower engines. They also utilize global positioning systems, satellite telephones, and other high tech devices to provide a seamless cocaine delivery system to the United States, the top consumer of cocaine in the world.

Smuggling people into the United States is a very profitable enterprise that also utilizes "mother ships" and fast boats. Smuggling humans has earned the smugglers thirty-two billion dollars worldwide in 2006. Southwest Florida has become a key area of concern with regards to Western Hemisphere human trafficking resulting in heavier patrols of the Florida Keys. With each person paying $ 8,000 to $ 10,000 to get to American soil, it is easy to understand the profits these modern day smugglers can accumulate.

Collier County, for example, has hundreds of miles of coastline, thousands of uninhabited islands and limited Federal enforcement agencies such as the Coast Guard, Border Patrol, or Immigration and Customs Enforcement. It is an ideal area, therefore, for Cuban migrant smugglers and other human traffickers to depart the local shores, pick up Cuban migrants or other nationalities, and make a quick return with their human cargoes.

Collier and Lee Counties have also become more accessible terminals since September 11, 2001 when the U. S. Navy and other Federal agencies strengthened border surveillance and detection efforts off the Florida Keys, making that area less attractive for the smugglers. Most of the current human smugglers bring their boats on trailers from the Miami area, launch them at area boat ramps and marinas, and complete their mission by going out to the mother ship and bringing the illegal migrants back to shore. They then return to the East Coast of Florida with their human cargo and a large profit.

Politics often create profits for those involved in human trafficking. Our current situation involving drug smuggling and human trafficking is in many ways similar to the Prohibition days of the Florida Rumrunners. The biggest supporters of Prohibition were the local moonshiners who profited from the law itself. In today's world we need to determine who benefits and profits by the drug and human smuggling. To solve these problems will take a study and a different approach other than relying solely on law enforcement agencies.

We have read the chapters that have taken us from the historical romance of Southwest Florida pirates, legend and fact through the reality of the barbarism that today's "pirates" employ in their quest for wealth, power, and freedom.

We are often asked, does Piracy exist today? The answer is definitely yes. With 95% of the world's trade traveling by ship and such small crews to man them, in some parts of the world particularly in the Indian and Pacific Oceans, there are no shortage of targets for traditional piracy.

In Southwest Florida, the long-term answer is that we need to discuss, evaluate and probably change many of our laws in the area of drugs and immigration. For, the fact remains that piracy is always a reaction to or because of the laws and condition of the times and the money that can be made in response to those times.

As we have challenged students in our history classes, "always realize that in order to understand our future, it is necessary and vital to know our past history, both real and mythical."

Federal Drug Administration, http://www.usdoj.gov/dea/index.htm

Burnett, Gene M., *Florida's Past: People & Events That Shaped The State Volume 2*, Sarasota, FL, Pineapple Press, 1988, pages 84-87.

Husty, Denes, "Smugglers have centuries-old history in SW Florida," The News-Press, (August 6, 2007) pages A1, A10

Babson, Jennifer, "Cuban migrant smugglers find new launch spot," *Herald (Miami, FL) (May 16, 2005)*: NA. Junior Edition. Thomson Gale.

"Refugees speeding to U.S. Shores, St. Petersburg Times Online, http://www.sptimes.com/2005/06/06/news (June 6, 2005)

"Speedboats Are Traffickers' Tool of Choice, Tumaco, Columbia, Nov. 6, 2005, CBS News, http://www.CBSNews.com

Raffaele, Paul, *The Pirate Hunters*, Smithsonian, August, 2007.

Glossary

Aft—the back or stern of a vessel or ship.

Ahoy—a call used in hailing or calling out to a ship.

Anchor—a heavy object, usually made of iron, shaped with flukes and attached to a chain and lowered into the water to keep a ship from drifting.

Articles—(Articles of Confederation) is a contract signed by pirates before going on a voyage. The articles are the ship's rules and how each person will be paid or divide up any prize or booty.

Avast—simply means to "stop."

Bar or Sandbar—a sandbank or a shoal, often under shallow water, at the mouth of a harbor, bay, or sound.

Blockade—shutting off of a port or city to prevent anyone from getting in or out.

Booty—a prize or cargo taken from a captured or sunken ship.

Bow—the front part of a ship or boat.

Bowsprit—a heavy spar that points forward from the bow of a ship.

Brigantine—a two-masted sailing vessel that can be rigged with either square or fore and aft sails. Generally a shallow draft hulled vessel that could sail in shallow or deep waters avoiding capture.

Broadside—(two definitions in this book) 1. The simultaneous firing of all the cannons on one side of a ship at an enemy. And 2. A large sheet of paper printed on one side and used to convey a political message or news, often posted on poles, trees, and bulletin boards.

Buccaneers—pirates who operated in the Caribbean and around the coast of South America during the 17th century. Original buccaneers were hunters from what is now Haiti and the Dominican Republic. Mostly French, they cooked their meat over open stoves in a process that was termed "boucaner" which gave these men their name.

Careen—to intentionally beach a ship, lay it over and remove the barnacles and seaweed from the hull.

Cobblestone—a rounded stone used as ballast in sailing ships and for paving streets.

Colors—the flags flown on ships to show what country they come from.

Corsairs—pirates based in the Mediterranean Sea. Generally, these corsairs were of the Muslim faith; however, the Corsairs of Malta were supported by Christians to fight the Muslim corsairs.

Cowboys—a term given to the colonists who remained loyal to England for the way in which they robbed or stole livestock from the 'rebels' or colonists fighting against England. The valuables taken or the livestock were sold or given to the British Army.

Doubloon—a gold Spanish coin.

Fathom—a measure of six feet in length used to define the depth of water.

Flukes—on dolphins, two adjacent horizontal flat appendages act like a paddle propelling the dolphin through the water with every up and down flex of the tail muscle.

Fore—the front part of a ship at the bow.

Forecastle—the upper deck of a ship in front of the foremast.

Frigate—a fast, three masted square rigged navy ship carrying between 24 and 40 cannons.

Galley—the kitchen of a ship.

Gangplank—a moveable bridge used in boarding or leaving a ship at a pier or dock.

Hull—the frame or body of a ship, without sails or rigging.

Immigrant—a person who immigrates to a new country or region.

Jolly Roger—A pirate ship's flag. Can have either a red or black background with symbols of death, like skull and crossbones.

Key—in the geographical sense, a reef or low island.

Legend—a story handed down for generations among a people and popularly believed to have a historical basis that is not verifiable.

Letter of Marque—a contract, license, or a commission issued by a government authorizing private vessels to attack and capture all ships of an enemy nation.

Longboat (Ship's Boat)—Generally the largest boat belonging to a ship that is used to carry heavy items and crewmembers to and from the ship.

Loyalist (Tories)—an American colonist upholding the cause of the British crown or remaining loyal to England during the American Revolution.

Man-of-War—an armed warship, generally a large one, used by the navy of a country with a national navy.

Merchant vessel (Merchantman)—a ship that transports goods and items used in commerce.

Patriots (Rebels)—During the American Revolution, those colonists who declared their independence from England and fought to form a new United States of America.

Piece of Eight—a Spanish coin used throughout the American colonies during the time of the American Revolution. Actually was our first currency. Term came from silver coins called cobs or pesos.

Pirates—men and women who loved freedom and robbed and plundered at sea and land to earn a living. They believed in democracy and equality.

Pod—a group of dolphins who live together.

Port—the left side of a ship as you face forward toward the bow.

Privateers—Armed privately owned ships, including the captain and crew, authorized by a commission or "Letter of Marque" by one country to attack and capture ships of an enemy country.

Prohibition—in our text, the forbidding by Federal law of the manufacture, transportation, or sale of alcoholic beverages during the period of 1920-1933.

Quarter Deck—a deck above the main deck at the stern (back) of the ship from where the captain and other officers control the ship.

Ratline—ropes forming the steps of a series of rope ladders running from the hull of a ship up the different masts.

Rigging—the arrangement of sails and masts on a ship.

Scuttle—to sink or attempt to sink a ship by cutting a whole in the hull.

Smuggler—to bring into or out of a country illegally is to smuggle. One who does this is called a "smuggler"

Squadron—a naval unit consisting of two or more divisions and sometimes additional vessels.

Square Rigged—sails set at right angles from horizontal yards attached to a mast of a ship.

Starboard—the right side of a ship as you face forward toward the bow.

Stern—the rear or back of a ship or boat.

Swivel Gun—small cannon that is mounted on a swivel, and mounted on the rail or from the fighting tops of vessels.

Sweet Trade—the name given to the practice of piracy, one of the oldest professions in the entire world.

Treasure—accumulated or stored (hidden) wealth in the form of money, jewels, precious metals or other valuables.

Yard—a long spar (wood) suspended from the mast of a ship to extend the sails.

Bibliography

"Alderman Held Criminal Record in Fort Myers, At One Time Acted As Fishing Guide for President Roosevelt, Fort Myers Tropical News, Fort Myers, FL, January 28, 1928.

American Folklore and Legend, Pleasantville, NY, The Reader's Digest Association, 1978.

Anholt, Betty, *Sanibel's Story, Voices and Images*, The Donnelly Co. Publishers, 1998.

Ans, Andre-Marcel d', *The Legend of Gasparilla: Myth and History on Florida's West Coast*, Tampa Bay History, 1980.

Babson, Jennifer, "Cuban migrant smugglers find new launch spot," *Herald (Miami, FL) (May 16, 2005)*: NA. Junior Edition. Thomson Gale.

Beater, Jack, *Pirates and Buried Treasure on Florida Islands*, St. Petersburg: Great Outdoors Publishing Co., 1959.

Bickel, Karl A., *The Mangrove Coast: The Story of the West Coast of Florida*, Coward-McCann, New York, 1942.

Buker, George E., *"Blockaders, refugees, and contrabands: civil war on Florida's Gulf Coast, 1861-1865,"* Tuscaloosa, Alabama: The University of Alabama Press, 1993.

Burnett, Gene M., *Florida's Past: People & Events That Shaped The State Volume 2*, Sarasota, FL, Pineapple Press, 1988.

Caudle, Hal M., *The Hanging at Bahia Mar*, Fort Lauderdale: Wake-Brook House, 1976.

Cordingly, David, *Under the Black Flag*, Random House, New York, New York, 1995.

"Despite embargo, U.S. top food source for island," *The News-Press (Ft. Myers, FL) (March 26, 2007)*.

Federal Drug Administration, http://www.usdoj.gov/dea/index.htm

Grismer, Karl H., The *Story of Fort Myers*, A Southwest Florida Historical Society Book, Fort Myers Beach: The Island Publishers, 1982.

Handbook of Texas Online, s.v.".," http://www.tsha.utexas.edu/handbook/online/articles/LL/fla12.html

Husty, Denes, "Smugglers have centuries-old history in SW Florida," The News-Press, (August 6, 2007).

McCarthy, Kevin M., *Nine Florida Stories by Marjory Stoneman Douglas*, Jacksonville: University of North Florida Press, 1990.

Raffaele, Paul, *The Pirate Hunters*, Smithsonian, August, 2007.

Rediker, Marcus, *Villains of All Nations*, Beacon Press, Boston, MA, 2004.

"Refugees speeding to U.S. Shores, St. Petersburg Times Online, http://www.sptimes.com/2005/06/06/news (June 6, 2005

Schell, Rolfe F., *1,000 Years on Mound Key*, Island Press, Ft. Myers, Fl., 1962.

"Speedboats Are Traffickers' Tool of Choice, Tumaco, Columbia, Nov. 6, 2005, CBS News, http://www.CBSNews.com

The Story of Jean and Pierre Lafitte, the Pirate-Patriots, New Orleans: Louisiana State Museum/Press of T. J. Moran's Sons, 1938.

About the Authors

James F. Kaserman is a retired educator and businessman and served in elected public office for more than ten years. Following graduation from Washington High School in Massillon, Ohio, he earned a bachelor's degree in business administration from Kent State University and a master's degree in educational administration from the University of Dayton. He was honorably discharged with the rank of staff sergeant from the United States Army.

Kaserman has been a newspaper columnist and served as a teacher, coach, and administrator for thirty-six years in both Ohio and Florida. He became interested in the truth about pirates when doing research studies of government and business organizations, and concluded that pirate organizations had many similarities to the businesses of today and even served as models for our modern day democracy.

Sarah Jane (Chenot) Kaserman an educator for over thirty-five years and recently retired as a teacher of gifted students in the Lee County School District in Florida. Following graduation from North Canton Hoover High School in North Canton, Ohio, she earned a bachelor's degree in Elementary Education and a master's degree in deaf education from Kent State University. A violinist and avid fiddle player, Sarah Jane arranged and played fiddle for a civil war movie, "The Miracle Men." She also travels the country and plays old-time, folk, and bluegrass music. She belongs to a Florida acoustic folk group entitled, "The Lee County Fiddle Support Group as well as other groups throughout the year. Sarah Jane and her grandfather's fiddle, "Charley" can be found at all presentations the Kaserman's put on regarding their series of pirate novels.

Together, they have combined their years in education with the vision of writing multi-sensory books and have written many elementary Accelerated Reader books that may be purchased through http://www.isaveatree.com They also have written three pirate novels, Gasparilla Pirate Genius, The Legend of Gasparilla, A Tale for All Ages; and, How the Pirates Saved Christmas. Each of these novels won awards and were good sellers.

They have been happily married since 1966 and are the parents of two sons, Richard and James, grandparents to James Hunter and Reed Samuel, and have lived in Fort Myers, Florida, since 1985 moving from their native Ohio.

978-0-595-47152-2
0-595-47152-8

Printed in the United States
97188LV00005B/58-75/A